What people are saying about
FROM THE Playground TO THE Battleground

What a beautiful reminder of the exhilarating joy of teaching (along with the challenges!) through our relationship and conversations with God. Michelle brings thoughtful, reflective, and yes, humorous ways of viewing the day-to-day of teaching God's wondrous gifts to us, our students. They matter. We matter. God is always with us.

—Dr. Trena L. Wilkerson, professor,
Department of Curriculum and Instruction
Chair, Baylor University, School of Education,
Department of Curriculum and Instruction

Michelle Ruddell nailed it! As a former middle school teacher, I found this book spoke straight to the heart of classroom life. Teaching is a calling filled with joy as well as exhaustion—all in the same day. She does not shy away from the real emotions we face. I highly recommend it to any teacher looking to blend purpose, patience, and prayer in their daily walk as they prepare to teach our leaders of tomorrow who are in their classrooms today.

—Tammy Whitehurst, motivational speaker,
author, and former teacher

The heart of a teacher is that of a warrior, born out of love and grit and faith. Michelle Ruddell's *From the Playground to the Battleground* captures all three with humor and unequivocal grace. Her words serve as a daily lifeline to those in the classroom trenches, pointing our way back to joy and reminding our hearts what we do matters for eternity.

—Sara Cormany, former educator and award-winning author of *Even When: Experiencing God's Presence During Difficult Days*

FROM THE
Playground
TO THE
Battleground

Finding Joy and Strength in the Classroom

40 DEVOTIONS FOR TEACHERS

© 2025 by Michelle Ruddell. All rights reserved.

Published by Redemption Press, 70 S. Val Vista Drive, Suite A3-442, Gilbert, AZ, 85296, (360) 226-3488.

Redemption Press is honored to present this title in partnership with the author. The views expressed or implied in this work are those of the author. Redemption Press provides our imprint seal representing design excellence, creative content, and high-quality production.

Noncommercial interests may reproduce portions of this book without the express written permission of the author, provided the text does not exceed five hundred words. When reproducing text from this book, include the following credit line: "From the *Playground to the Battleground: Finding Joy and Strength in the Classroom* by Michelle Ruddell. Used by permission."

No part of this publication may be reproduced in any form, stored in a retrieval system, or transmitted in any form by any means—electronic, photocopy, recording, or otherwise—without prior written permission of the publisher/author, except as provided by United States of America copyright law.

Unless otherwise indicated, all Scripture quotations are taken from the Holy Bible, New Living Translation, copyright © 1996, 2004, 2007 by Tyndale House Foundation. Used by permission of Tyndale House Publishers, Carol Stream, Illinois 60188. All rights reserved. Scripture quotations marked (NIV) are taken from the Holy Bible, New International Version®, NIV®. Copyright © 1973, 1978, 1984, 2011 by Biblica, Inc.™ Used by permission of Zondervan. All rights reserved worldwide. www.zondervan.com The "NIV" and "New International Version" are trademarks registered in the United States Patent and Trademark Office by Biblica, Inc.™

ISBN 13: 978-1-64645-946-9 (paperback)
978-1-64645-947-6 (ePub)

Library of Congress Catalog Card Number: 2025907458

FROM THE
Playground
TO THE
Battleground

Finding Joy and Strength in the Classroom

40 DEVOTIONS FOR TEACHERS

Michelle Ruddell
FOREWORD BY Brenda Parker

CONTENTS

Foreword 1
Letter to the Reader 3

1. Francisco 5
2. Like Christmas 8
3. In-Service Days 11
4. The Honeymoon Period 14
5. Getting to Know Students 17
6. Cheetos 20
7. Negativity Is Contagious 23
8. Tug-of-War 26
9. The October Slump 29
10. Peace with Everyone? 32
11. A Bottle of Water 35
12. The Beginning of the Grading Period 38
13. New Ideas 41
14. The Rough Days 44
15. Accountability and Grace 47
16. Is the Door Locked? 50
17. The Guinea Pig 53
18. The Countdown 56
19. Aha Moments 59
20. A New Semester 62

21	Where's Your Focus	65
22	Parent Contacts	68
23	Is the Door Locked? 2.0	71
24	Meetings, Meetings, and More Meetings	74
25	Celebrations	77
26	In His Strength	80
27	An Eye-Opening Experience	83
28	Clifford the Big Red Dog Day	86
29	Change in the Weather	89
30	Back to the Basics	92
31	Teacher Time Warp	95
32	The Plan	98
33	Parent Contacts 2.0	101
34	A Clean Slate	104
35	Jesus as Teacher	107
36	I Messed Up	110
37	Overwhelmed	113
38	Summer School	116
39	Summer School 2.0	119
40	Francisco 2.0	122

A Blessing for the Battleground 125
About the Author 127

Foreword

Seldom in my life have I felt as honored as I feel writing the foreword for this book of devotionals. Having worked in the educational arena for more than thirty-plus years, each devotion in this book touched chords of memories from those days of my career.

I have the privilege of knowing Michelle Ruddell from the beginning of her career to her second retirement from teaching. That privilege is not given often, and I do not think lightly of it. I have seen the heart of this author! The words written on these pages are words she has spoken to herself in the best of times and the worst of times.

Whether you are a new or a well-seasoned educator, this book will resonate with you! If it doesn't, well, hold on to the book, because it will! God doesn't let anything we experience go to waste, whether it be positive or negative. This book encapsulates decades (sorry, Michelle) of wisdom that God has inspired through some of the sweetest and the roughest of his children. We would be wise to allow this book to awaken our hearts, minds, and spirits to the lessons that God teaches us as we teach others.

I hope you enjoy reading and pondering these life lessons as much as I have. I think you will find that they will take you from the playground to the battleground, and then to the playground once again!

Prayerfully,
Brenda Parker
Matthew 25:34–40

Letter to the Reader

To my fellow education warriors:

I see the struggle of long days and ever-changing requirements. I feel the exhaustion of working long hours to keep up with tasks that fit only past the last bell. I sense the burden of stretching your paycheck to cover the most basic of bills. I hear you when you say you lie awake at night, burdened by a kid's heart-wrenching story or searching for a way to reach *that* student. I see you zoned out during your planning period, gathering just enough energy for the next class. I see you, I hear you, and I know you—because I've been there too.

When we played school as kids, these challenges weren't even on our radar. Our "students" were well behaved and eager to learn. There were no discipline problems, meetings, or documentation to manage. We loved children and wanted to change the world, so we became teachers. Now our delight in teaching is sometimes overshadowed by stress. What we once envisioned as a playground has become a battleground on many fronts.

Is it still possible to find joy in education? I believe it is. Now more than ever, our students need to know they are seen and valued. Lightbulb moments and the thrill they bring are still there. The delight of connection is still there. The satisfaction of discovering what turns struggle into success is still there.

My hope for you as you read these pages is that you will find the laughter, encouragement, and inspiration you need to stay in the fight. It is also my hope that you will relish the playground moments and gain strength for the battle. Because what you do matters. What you say matters. What you give matters. *You* matter. Both to me and to the One who called you into this profession. He will equip you and carry you through the tough days. He will delight in and rejoice with you on the good days. And he will hold you and keep you on all the days.

From the playground to the battleground, he is with you, and so is my heart.

Michelle

1

Francisco

> *"My thoughts are nothing like your thoughts," says the Lord. "And my ways are far beyond anything you could imagine. For just as the heavens are higher than the earth, so my ways are higher than your ways and my thoughts higher than your thoughts."*
>
> ISAIAH 55:8–9

I will *never* forget Francisco.

It was my first day of teaching; and as I did my best to quash my nerves, in he walked. Plopping his foot onto a chair and hiking up his pant leg, he loudly announced, "I can't wait to get this thing off!"

It was the first time I had ever seen a probation department ankle monitor. Trying to hide my shock, I threw back a casual, "I bet you can't."

But as I walked out into the hallway to greet my other students, I silently prayed, *God, are you sure this is where I'm supposed to be? My diploma says elementary education, but this is an alternative high school. My specialization is English, and I'm supposed to teach these teenagers home economics. I barely cook, I don't sew, and I only clean when it's critical—so that might be a problem. This was not what I envisioned when I thought about being a teacher. I'm in over my head.*

I won't begin to pretend I had no difficulty and doubt in this year of firsts. I experienced overload from multiple subjects, a mountain of grading, and heartbreak over the hard stories my students carried. But there was also unexpected delight in my first year. I learned to build relationships with students, discovered the thrill of the aha moments, and learned to love the sound of "Mrs. Ruddell."

Although I often felt ill-equipped to fight the battles I faced, I knew God had placed me in that school for a reason. I also knew I had to depend on him to function in this role. There were battleground moments when I questioned God's assignment for me, and there were playground moments when I stood in awe of his blessings.

As with every area of life, the classroom will place us in situations we don't plan or expect. But even when we are in over our heads, we can trust God to provide for us and equip us for every assignment he has given us. For he who called us is always faithful (1 Thessalonians 5:24).

REFLECT: What moments have led you to ask God, "Are you sure this is where I'm supposed to be?"

REFOCUS: God's ways are higher than ours. We can trust him when we feel ill-equipped. We can claim peace even in our fear. And we can depend on him to guide us through uncharted territory.

Heavenly Father,
Thank you for having plans for us that are bigger than our expectations. Thank you for equipping us to do even what we doubt in our own strength. Help us to trust you as we walk into the unfamiliar and may the steps we take be lined with humble obedience.
In Jesus' name,
Amen.

2

Like Christmas

Great is his faithfulness; his mercies begin afresh each morning.
LAMENTATIONS 3:23

Every summer, a switch in my brain flips on. One moment I'm in the middle of the local superstore audibly muttering, "*Ugh*, not back-to-school stuff yet." Then, before you know it, I'm headed straight for the #2 pencils, gleefully exclaiming, "Look! School supplies!"

Like a child waiting for Santa, I eagerly anticipate the beginning of a new school year. Boxes of dry-erase markers and gel pens are delivered to my front porch. Blank composition books and new folders fill my cart at the store. Everything is fresh and new.

Even before in-service begins, I sneak into my classroom. The whiteboards are sparkling, the floors are clean, and there isn't one stack of paper on my desk. Logging into my gradebook, I hope for a peek at my rosters. A whole list of unfamiliar names stares back at me. *What will this new group of students be like?* Like presents under the tree, I wonder what surprises await.

Teaching is unique in that there is a fresh start every year.

We meet a new group of students, build new relationships, and establish new routines. We've left our frustration with the old year behind and feel ready to meet new challenges. We've had a break to rest and recharge. Now it's time to start again.

As you face the beginning of a new school year, remember it is more like a playground than a battleground. Soak up that joy. Use it for strength. The battle is coming.

REFLECT: How does the beginning of a new school year make you feel?

REFOCUS: Leave the failures and shortcomings of last year in the past. Allow yourself the grace of a fresh start. Stand ready to give others the same.

Heavenly Father,
Thank you for the grace of a new beginning. May we lean into the excitement and joy it can bring. And may we look to you as the author of new mercies, second chances, and fresh starts.
In Jesus' name,
Amen.

3

In-Service Days

Work willingly at whatever you do, as though you were working for the Lord rather than for people.

COLOSSIANS 3:23

Once upon an in-service day, a teacher walked into her bright, shiny classroom with a spring in her step. She organized her room. She planned her lessons. She caught up with coworkers. And by the end of the day, she left feeling rested and relaxed because her room was ready to go.

That sounds like a fairy tale, right?

In the real world, there are required meetings and training to complete. There's probably also a data meeting and some grade-level or vertical planning to be done. And then there's always the delightful motivational speaker.

When we walk into professional development days at the beginning of the year, chances are we fall into one of these three categories:

- ✔ The teacher who is happy to be there and is talking to everybody.
- ✔ The teacher who is happy to be back but can't focus because there are a million things on her classroom to-do list.
- ✔ The teacher who is mourning the end of her summer.

The behind-the-scenes work of education isn't always the most fun and exciting. I've seen administrators go to great lengths to improve the appeal of those days, yet their efforts never seem to please everybody.

What is your strategy for in-service days? Do you grin and bear it, counting the minutes until lunch or the end of the day? Do you complain to everyone around you about how you'd rather be in your room?

Imagine if we turned the script around, viewing these days as a necessity even if we struggle to recognize it. Imagine if we walked into each session looking for one idea that might make classroom life easier. Imagine if we saw ourselves as trendsetters when we hear an idea in training that we've already implemented.

Negativity during in-service days can turn the playground-like excitement of a new year into a battleground of I-don't-want-to-be-here. It can sap your energy and bring down the excitement of those around you. But when we are working as for the Lord, our attitude and our face should show it.

REFLECT: How do our leaders feel when we communicate clearly that we would rather be anywhere but here? Probably the same way we feel when our students are obviously disengaged.

REFOCUS: Walk into in-service days looking for the positive. Reflect the same attitude you'd want in your own classroom. Find ways to encourage those who've worked hard to serve you and your students.

Heavenly Father,
Thank you for those who continue to step up and step into this calling. Bless us as we sit through necessary meetings that sometimes seem more like a battleground than a playground. Give us open hearts and minds as we find ways to improve the classroom experience for our students.
In Jesus' name,
Amen.

4

The Honeymoon Period

> *So now we can rejoice in our wonderful new relationship with God because our Lord Jesus Christ has made us friends of God.*
> ROMANS 5:11

Standing back with the confidence that comes at the beginning of a school year, I admired my new, neon-colored word wall. Nothing was going to keep me from believing I would switch out words with each new unit. I did my best to drown out past experience that knew the same words would be on the wall at the end of the grading period, the end of the semester, and the end of the year.

The euphoria that comes with a new year is fleeting. Soon enough, the day-to-day grind would send me back to survival mode. But in that moment, I tried to ignore my inner voice of self-doubt: *You won't be able to keep up. Those words for Unit 1 will still be there at Christmas. Shh. I'm not listening to that negativity today. This year is going to be different.*

The sense of invincibility at the beginning of the school year is unique. We need to learn to savor it, knowing it won't last. All too soon, the hamster wheel of grades and plans and materials prep will start.

But in the moment, the immediate to-do list is done. Students are following the routines and procedures. The new will wear off, but not today, leaving most of us to wonder, *Can we bottle this new feeling and bring it out in April?*

The start of a new semester is like the start of a new relationship. We are smitten with what might be, with what is possible. We haven't yet gotten bogged down in the day-to-day routines and stresses.

The energy and joy of the new school year provide a playground moment. These memories give us strength to carry us through the battleground days. We need to protect the spark of that newness in preparation for the days when joy is hard won.

REFLECT: What is it that excites you the most at the beginning of a new school year?

_____
_____
_____
_____
_____
_____
_____
_____
_____
_____
_____
_____
_____
_____

REFOCUS: Soak up the joy of the honeymoon period at the start of a new school year. Take advantage of the energy boost. Enjoy the creativity that can surface before the day-to-day pace saps your energy.

Heavenly Father,
Thank you for the fresh start of a new school year. Bless each teacher, staff member, and administrator as they step into the new beginning. Give them joy in their work and delight in you. Guide each word, each action, and each decision made. May you be glorified in all that we do.
In Jesus' name,
Amen.

5

Getting to Know Students

> *So now I am giving you a new commandment: Love each other. Just as I have loved you, you should love each other. Your love for one another will prove to the world that you are my disciples.*
>
> JOHN 13:34–35

"Mrs. Ruddell, this is your new student, Craig."

Craig was the newest member of my intervention class, consisting of a small group of middle school students who needed extra help in math. Gaining their trust and building their confidence was a balancing act, and adding a new student to the mix could tip the scales I had worked so hard to balance.

On his second day in our group, Craig walked up behind me and clapped his hands together right behind my head. My ears rang as my temper rose. Craig, however, thought it was hilarious.

Over the next few weeks, this child refused to work, disrupted the class, and continued to disrespect me. I could almost see the wheels turning in the heads of my other students as they chose sides. I had to figure this out, or we were all going to be miserable.

Craig's other math teacher and I tag teamed. We held him accountable for his behavior while using strategies to find and address his academic struggles. We communicated with his coaches, who helped us encourage appropriate classroom behavior, and we celebrated small wins.

I'm convinced that Craig's initial behavior was his attempt to fit in and find his place in a new school. As he figured out that these two crazy math teachers cared enough to help him and hold him accountable for his behavior, his whole demeanor changed. We saw his sense of humor and his positive leadership. He became an active participant in working through his academic struggles.

A former principal of mine often referenced this quote: "They won't care how much you know until they know how much you care."[1] Sometimes it's hard to convince students that we can hold them accountable for behavior and assignments and care about them at the same time.

Understanding that there is always a story behind behavior helps us to know how to address it. It does *not* mean we allow students to be disruptive and disrespectful. But what it does tell us is that truly knowing our students is a battle-ready strategy. The better we know them, the better prepared we can be for the tough days.

REFLECT: How can you let students know that you want the best for them even when you are holding them accountable?

_____
_____
_____
_____
_____

---

1. Often attributed to Theodore Roosevelt, but no source can verify this attribution. It has become well-known and frequently used.

REFOCUS: God knows you. He cares for you. See your students through his eyes.

Heavenly Father,
Thank you for the blessing and privilege of getting to know a new group of students each year. Help us to see them as you do. Give us wisdom and discernment as we build relationships with our new students. Teach us how to connect with them and guide them as you would have us do.
In Jesus' name,
Amen.

6

Cheetos

> *A cheerful heart is good medicine, but a broken spirit saps a person's strength.*
> PROVERBS 17:22

It was the first day of class, and my new darlings were busily using their cell phones to respond to a poll. Their answers, which were anonymous, showed up on the screen at the front of the room. Some of these questions were just for fun. Others gave me an idea as to how these students learned best. All of them helped me know them better.

In one class a trend appeared.

What is your favorite snack? Cheetos.

How do you learn best? With Cheetos.

What makes a good learning environment for you? Cheetos.

What do you want to be when you grow up? Cheetos.

The giggles became belly laughs as we bonded over it all, which got my teacher-senses tingling. These students had given me a clear path to getting on their good side. As soon as the last bell rang, I shoved my own children into our minivan and headed for the grocery store. The moment we arrived, I headed straight to the chip aisle and grabbed two of the biggest bags of Cheetos I could find.

The following day, I grinned with excitement as I waited for that class period to arrive. As I stood at my door waiting for the bell to ring, I glanced into the classroom to discover my new favorite student beating me to the punch as I watched her quietly put a single Cheeto on each desk.

After announcing her contribution and thanking her, I pulled out the bags I had purchased from behind my desk and had volunteers pass out more of our new favorite snack. On their way out, one student looked at me and shook her head. "I can't believe you brought us Cheetos." I smiled and thought, *These cool-teacher points came too easily.*

We laughed about Cheetos all year long. I'm still in touch with one student from that class, and we often have a good laugh about Cheetos.

God gives us good gifts, yet we are often surprised when he does. But just like my students did with their creative answers, we can tell God our desires even as teachers.

During every school year, battleground moments will come. When you have a chance to create a playground moment, take advantage of it. Sometimes, it's as easy as a trip to the store for Cheetos.

REFLECT: How have you discovered a creative way to your students' good sides?

REFOCUS: Thank God for the gifts he gives. Take advantage of opportunities to surprise your students. Enjoy the unexpected connections.

Heavenly Father,
Help us to be aware of moments when we can provide good things for our students. Help us recognize and take advantage of playground moments when we can bring joy into the classroom. And help us to bring our desires to you and trust you to give us good things.
In Jesus' name,
Amen.

7

Negativity Is Contagious

Do everything without complaining and arguing.
PHILIPPIANS 2:14

Bebopping into school one August day, I heard a heavy sigh from a teacher walking behind me. I turned and faced her. "That's not an August sound. That's an *April* sound." Always excited for a fresh start, I couldn't imagine dreading school that much so early in the year.

Negativity is contagious. Sometimes the best way to win the battleground moments is to protect your perspective by avoiding negativity. It might mean staying away from certain people on your campus. It very well might mean bypassing the teacher's lounge.

Every day has both good and bad. Complaining rarely changes anything except the mood in the room. So be wary of complaining, even your own.

When something bad happens in your class, do you run during the passing period to tell your next-door teacher, and then in the next break, do you tell it to the teacher on the other side? It's tempting to participate in the *who-had-the-worst-day* story contest.

But as teachers, we know the value of repetition. It increases retention. Guess what happens when we tell our worst-day stories over and over? That's what we remember.

In a heartbeat, we can turn a playground moment into a battleground moment. But imagine if the stories we couldn't wait to share were stories of student success or a good class discussion. No doubt our perspective would be different.

We'd go from a who-had-the-worst-day story contest to who-had-the-best-day. And just like that, a battleground would be a playground. Scripture describes good news "like cold water to the thirsty" (Proverbs 25:25). Let's be bearers of good news every chance we get.

REFLECT: How can you guard your heart and mind against negativity?

REFOCUS: Protect your perspective. Avoid the worst-day story contest. Look for the good.

Heavenly Father,
Thank you for the choice to focus on the good. Help us to share the positive, even when we experience the negative. Help us to encourage our colleagues and to be bearers of good news.
In Jesus' name,
Amen.

8

Tug-of-War

> *I cling to you; your strong right hand holds me securely.*
>
> PSALM 63:8

Michelle, you can be the cool teacher. With nothing but my inner monologue cheering me on, I signed up to be a faculty participant in a game for the upcoming pep rally. With my daughter watching from the stands that day, the timing seemed perfect.

The morning of the pep rally quickly came, and as I reported to the gym floor, I felt confident I knew what was coming. Historically, teachers competed against the students. But I quickly discovered today would be different.

Each teacher volunteer was assigned to a group of students. My team? High school juniors. The game? Tug-of-war. I quickly found all five-foot-one of me sandwiched between a slew of varsity football players, grabbing hold of a rope, and praying not to die.

The whistle blew, the rope jerked, and my feet went out from under me. I clung to that rope as those boys pulled the other team across the line. Laughter started to slowly spread across the gym—once everybody knew I was alive.

Later my daughter asked me, "Why didn't you just let go?"

"Did you see those boys around me?" I chuckled. "My choice was to hang on and be dragged or let go and be trampled."

Sometimes hanging on for dear life is the best we can do. When school is a battleground, and you feel as inadequate as a five-foot-tall math teacher playing tug-of-war with football players, hang on to God with everything you've got.

He knows you. He loves you. And he will carry you now and all the days to come.

REFLECT: What school circumstances make you feel like the only options you have are being dragged or being trampled?

REFOCUS: Remember God's faithfulness in the past. Even on the difficult days, he promises to be with us. Trust him to keep that promise.

Heavenly Father,
Thank you for being the "rope" we can cling to even when life causes us to lose our footing and we feel as though we may be trampled. Help us to remember your faithfulness in the tough times. May the grace of laughter and humor meet us in the in-between.
In Jesus' name,
Amen.

9

The October Slump

> *But those who trust in the L*ORD *will find new strength.*
> *They will soar high on wings like eagles. They will run*
> *and not grow weary. They will walk and not faint.*
>
> ISAIAH 40:31

The newness of the school year has worn off. The constant cycle of planning, prepping, and grading wears you down. Evenings and weekends are spent on schoolwork or at school activities. You're struggling to keep your head above water. Thanksgiving break seems like a hundred years away. You're in full-on survival mode.

The students feel it too. They push boundaries and buttons and slack on their work. All hope of catching up is lost. Teachers and students are stressed and are getting on one another's nerves. Everyone is ready for a break.

When you're weary from the battleground days, cultivating playground moments can feel just beyond your bandwidth. What can you do to refresh and reenergize? May I give you the following suggestions?

Give your students a catch-up day. Take a break from packing lunch and order in, or skip cooking tonight and eat out. Leave your school bag in your classroom or in your car one night. Take a nap when you get home.

Some teachers de-stress by catching up on work. Extra rest refreshes others. Some restore hope by putting a countdown to the holiday on the board. The important thing is to do what works best for you.

Just remember the slump won't last forever. The next break will eventually come. Be patient with yourself and your students during the long stretch. While the span between breaks can be a battleground, patience, flexibility, and grace are winning strategies.

Like the wait for a holiday break, the wait for an answer from God can be a battle. When the season of struggle seems endless, we can trust him. He hasn't forgotten us; his plan and his timing are still perfect.

REFLECT: What are some signs that you are battle-weary and ready for a break?

REFOCUS: We know a break is coming. Our students feel the same stress. We can defuse the bomb or fan the flames—choose wisely.

Heavenly Father,
Thank you for sustaining us through long, difficult days, be it in the classroom or in life. Remind us that you are our strength and our hope always. Give us wisdom and encouragement to make it through the times when we feel like a break will never come.
In Jesus' name,
Amen.

10

Peace with Everyone?

> *Make every effort to live in peace with everyone and to be holy; without holiness no one will see the Lord.*
>
> HEBREWS 12:14 (NIV)

A crowd of high school students swirled around me, rushing between classes. Trying my best to hold back tears, I stood at my door, holding my breath until I could step into my classroom and let the weight of emotions hit. It was *finally* my planning period.

As the hallway began to clear, I noticed a scrap of index card on the floor. *Someone might need that,* I thought, as I picked it up and turned it over to read: "Make every effort to live in peace with everyone and to be holy; without holiness no one will see the Lord."

Peace with everyone? I struggled with the thought, especially knowing the source of my frustration. The flexibility that had worked so well with my alternative school students was failing miserably in my first year at a traditional high school.

My new students interpreted my flexibility as an inability to set boundaries and stick to them. The truth is, they weren't wrong. I was afraid to ask for help and let the other teachers know I was in over my head.

Every part of me wanted to quit; but when God gives you a job across the state through an over-the-phone interview from a hospital bed, quitting might get you swallowed by a big fish.[2]

How could I learn to live in peace with these kids? Simply put, I had to embrace my role by making every effort.

Making every effort meant learning the strategies and approaches that worked for my students. Making every effort meant setting boundaries and sticking to them. Making every effort included swallowing my pride and asking for help from other teachers and administrators. The bottom line: *I needed to make every effort if I was ever going to truly live in peace.*

In that battleground moment, I wanted to wave the white flag. But God gave me the strength and guidance to call in reinforcements, ask for help, and keep battling. Don't let fear or pride cause you to surrender in your battleground moments. Instead, make every effort to bring peace, transforming your battleground back into a playground.

REFLECT: What classroom circumstances are tempting you to wave the white flag?

___

2. Jonah 1:1–17

REFOCUS: Peace in the classroom begins with us. On the days we want to quit, God will walk with us. And he will reveal what we need to do to make every effort.

Heavenly Father,
Be with us as we march into battle. May we strive to set boundaries and expectations. Grant us the wisdom to deal with students who disregard them. And give us the humility to ask for help when we need it.
In Jesus' name,
Amen.

11

A Bottle of Water

> *But those who drink the water I give will never be thirsty again. It becomes a fresh, bubbling spring within them, giving them eternal life.*
>
> JOHN 4:14

"Mrs. Ruddell, can I go to the bathroom?"

In case you are not fluent in high-school-student speak, this phrase can mean any one of the following:

- ✔ Can I roam the halls?
- ✔ Can I go meet my friends?
- ✔ Can I go use my phone?
- ✔ Can I go hang out in another teacher's class?

One particular year, I had a student, Shyanna, who quickly figured out I had decoded her "Can I go to the bathroom?" question. In her case, what it really meant was she needed to roam the halls to check on the drama of the day. My answer quickly became a standard no.

Not to be outdone, she switched her tactics. "Mrs. Ruddell, can I please go get a drink of water?"

Far be it from me to deprive a poor, parched student of a drink of water. My next move, however, beat her at her own game. "Here's a new, unopened bottle of water for you. You can have it."

With that move I was caring and strategic. She wouldn't be thirsty, and she would have to stay in class. For several days, the pattern continued until she finally caught on.

"Mrs. Ruddell, are you giving me water every day to keep me in the classroom?"

I smiled. "You figured it out."

This could have been a battleground moment. Shyanna wanted out of the classroom, and her method was asking for a drink. If I had just said no every day, she could have (and would have) argued about how thirsty she was and how I needed to let her get a drink, and she was dehydrated, etc., etc.

Many students use this tactic. By giving Shyanna a water bottle when she was thirsty, I created a connection and what eventually became a playground moment. Years later, we still laugh about that day.

In the same way, when we ask God for something, do we trust his provision? Often he meets our needs in ways we never could have imagined. We may not even recognize the protection he is offering us in his answer. But he is faithful, and he is always for us.

REFLECT: Who is your "water-bottle" student? How can you connect with them in an unexpected way?

REFOCUS: Look for the need that lies behind a student's request. Find a creative way to meet that need. And trust that God will honor your efforts.

Heavenly Father,
Thank you for your faithfulness in provision and protection. Thank you for hearing our requests and for meeting our needs according to your perfect will. Help us as teachers to meet the needs of our students in ways that are best for them and help us to learn from them.
In Jesus' name,
Amen.

12

The Beginning of the Grading Period

> *And I will give them singleness of heart and put a new spirit within them. I will take away their stony, stubborn heart and give them a tender, responsive heart.*
>
> EZEKIEL 11:19

If I stay up until midnight or get up at four in the morning, I can get those papers graded. If I'd taught that lesson differently, more students would have been successful. What else could I have done to get that student to turn in his or her work?

The end of the grading period can bring on an onslaught of teacher guilt. We second-guess our efforts. We plead and we prod, we accommodate and adjust. We pull every tool from our Mary-Poppins-like teacher bag of tricks. And we question if it is enough.

But then—the clock strikes. The deadline is here. The negotiations are over. It is finished. A new grading period has dawned. Now my teacher-conscience is clear. The students' slate is clean. We start over. No one is behind.

A new grading period for teachers and students can give us the same feeling as the beginning of a new year. It's a symbol of a fresh start, and it's a marker of progress in the school year.

That new grading period mirrors life. A weight is lifted when we turn the page on the old and start fresh in the new. There's a sense of freedom in knowing that the struggle of the past is over and we have a chance to begin again.

That's what Jesus offers. Forgiveness of past sins and a clean, fresh start. He also gives us help and guidance for each step of the way. May we offer the same to those he places in our classroom and care.

REFLECT: Where do you need a fresh start?

REFOCUS: It's never too late to turn the page on old ways. We don't have to wait for a new grading period for a fresh start with Jesus; his mercies are new every morning (Lamentations 3:23).

Heavenly Father,
Thank you for forgiveness of the past and a chance to start again. Thank you for paying the penalty for all our failures. Thank you for a fresh, new page. Help us to fill it with obedience to you and successful completion of the tasks you assign us.
In Jesus' name,
Amen

13

New Ideas

> *Your own ears will hear him. Right behind you a voice will say, "This is the way you should go," whether to the right or to the left.*
> ISAIAH 30:21

Sitting at a conference surrounded by other math teachers, I balked a bit at the claim of another attendee. "My students race into the room before the tardy bell so they can get to the board to have first choice at the day's math problems!"

Even in my skepticism, I'll admit I was also intrigued. Instead of taking up homework and grading it every day, she put selected problems from the assignment on the board. As students came into the classroom, they went to the board and worked a problem of their choosing.

"Some days we only go over some problems; some days we go over all the problems. Students get immediate feedback, I can answer questions, and they can correct their work on their papers. I give them two five-question quizzes each week from those problems, but I don't take up their homework and grade it every day."

I liked the idea of students at the board, working together and having math conversations. I also liked the idea of not grading stacks of papers every day. I left that conference fired up and ready to try this new idea.

Like many dreamy-days-of-summer plans, I chickened out when it came time to go back to work. I was worried that my kids wouldn't buy in and that my great idea would flop. I decided to stick with the status quo.

But all that changed the moment I saw my rosters: 135 names. There was no way I could keep up and give my students next-day feedback. I was overwhelmed, and school hadn't even started. I had to give this new idea a try.

What started as a solution to my grading problem quickly became a game changer for my students. Soon they were rushing in before the tardy bell, grabbing a marker, and choosing the problem that they wanted to solve. They grew in their confidence to work problems and explain their thinking.

For the first time, the students had ownership of their work. The board was a safe place to make mistakes, and we worked together to correct misconceptions and misunderstandings. I stepped into this new class procedure with a lot of doubt but also saw benefits I never expected.

Sometimes God leads us to do things that we aren't sure of, things that are outside of our comfort zones. When we follow his lead even in that uncertainty, it leads to blessings beyond what we could have ever imagined. Trying new methods in the classroom can be a battle-winning strategy. Sometimes it takes facing a giant (like 135 students) to give us courage to make the switch.

REFLECT: Where have you tried a new routine in your classroom that worked well?

_____

_____

_____

_____

_____

_____

_____

REFOCUS: Think of a new idea or a tweak to an old one that you can try. Resist the urge to chicken out. Watch as the unexpected benefits appear.

> *Heavenly Father,*
> *Thank you for the new ideas that we get from coworkers, books, and experts. Help us to know which ones would benefit our students or make our jobs easier. Give us the courage to try new things and trust you in them.*
> *In Jesus' name,*
> *Amen.*

14

The Rough Days

> *I have told you all this so that you may have peace in me.*
> *Here on earth, you will have many trials and sorrows.*
> *But take heart because I have overcome the world.*
>
> JOHN 16:33

The honeymoon period doesn't last forever. As exciting as the new year is, at some point our students will test us. They will push every button we've got and make us question our sanity.

Student behavior is not the only contributor to rough days. Conflicts with coworkers or supervisors, disruptions to schedules, or outside-of-school circumstances can stretch us to our limit. When we take that stress level home, we might be tempted to snap at our family members or kick the dog.

On one such day, I sat at my desk trying to compose myself before my own children arrived after school. I needed to contact some parents, but where to start? The list of joy-stealers that day was long.

Then the thought of another student crossed my mind. When faced with the choice of joining his friends in shenanigans, he chose to separate himself. I decided to email his parents and compliment him on his choice.

"I am writing to brag on your student today. He made a good choice and stayed out of the disruptive behavior his friends were participating in. I appreciate his respect and his effort. Please tell him thank you for me."

I was surprised at how much better I felt. I thought of another student who had made good choices that day. I emailed her parents. Focusing on the positive changed my mood and my mindset before I went home. My kids and my dog were happier too.

This became my practice for all the rough days. I couldn't avoid dealing with negative student behavior, but before I went home, I would send some positive emails or make some positive phone calls. Some days one or two was enough. Some days it took five. One day, I made ten.

Rough days are battleground days. Sometimes we feel like we are losing. But we can deal with the hard stuff without taking the battle home.

REFLECT: Have you made a habit of taking the stress of the rough days home with you?

REFOCUS: Protect the home field. Find a way to be proactive about changing your mindset before you walk through the door. Leave the school battles at school.

Heavenly Father,
Give us wisdom to deal with the rough days. Help us to follow your example when dealing with circumstances and situations that are frustrating, unfair, and difficult. Help us to remember to be thankful for the good days and learn from the rough ones.
In Jesus' name,
Amen.

15

Accountability and Grace

> *Out of his fullness we have all received grace in place of grace already given.*
>
> JOHN 1:16 (NIV)

"Why am I failing, Mrs. Ruddell?"

"You have six zeros, sir."

Even with an extension, offered tutorials, and class time to work, this student-athlete still had six zeros. I attributed his lack of effort to the fact that football season was over, and his motivation for passing the class was gone. I even tried calling his mom, but she was just as frustrated.

When the grading period ended, he still had six zeros and a failing grade for the nine weeks. But I soon learned that besides being a talented football player, he was an important part of the track team. A failing grade meant he couldn't participate and would miss an important meet.

I had offered grace to this student before the grading period ended by extending due dates and being available for tutorials. He didn't accept either of those opportunities. His refusal brought a hefty consequence, and he was held accountable.

Grace *after* the missed track meet was a conversation where I expressed my confidence in his ability to pass the next nine weeks and offered to help. He had a change of heart. He completed assignments and turned them in on time. Not only did he pass the next nine weeks and the semester, he also learned from his mistakes and changed his behavior.

As teachers, we strive to maintain a delicate balance between accountability and grace. Our hearts want to give second chances, and third, and fourth. But we know that we also must hold our students accountable, as they often learn more from failure than they do from infinite chances.

Even as adults, we are sometimes like my failing athlete. We refuse the help that's offered or fail to do what God has told us to do. We often fall short and suffer the consequences of our choices. But because of his grace, we can learn from our failures, ask for forgiveness, and start again.

REFLECT: How do you balance accountability and grace with your students?

REFOCUS: Accountability is necessary for our students' success. Grace is a battle-winner. Balancing the two is an art.

> *Heavenly Father,*
> *Thank you for the grace you offer. Thank you for giving us second chances. When we suffer the consequences of our choices, help us turn to you for mercy and grace.*
> *In Jesus' name,*
> *Amen.*

16

Is the Door Locked?

> *You will keep in perfect peace all who trust in you, all whose thoughts are fixed on you!*
>
> ISAIAH 26:3

A shiver ran down my spine as the heavy gate clanged shut behind me. A swipe of my badge unlocked the door to the building. I juggled my bag, my lunch, and my water so I could reach the key on my lanyard to unlock the classroom door. *Am I at a middle school or a prison?*

Three times between the car and the classroom, I faced the reminder that our safety wasn't certain. *This.* This was why teaching was harder than it used to be. Would the locked gate and two locked doors keep my students safe?

The question every time someone entered or left my room became *Is the door locked?* If I forgot to check attendance, a quick phone call from the front desk served as a reminder, but if I forgot to lock the door? We might fail the audit. We might have to go through training. Or we might have to deal with something far worse.

Is the door locked?

In lockdown drills, administrators walked through the halls. They checked classroom doors. The jiggle of the handle put me on alert, even when I knew it was a drill.

Will I ever have to do this when it's not a drill?

The reality that one day a lockdown might not be a drill is ever present for educators. All the normal stressors like classroom management, lesson plans, and grades pile on top of the concern for student safety.

We have some control over normal conditions. We can get better at classroom management. We can learn how to plan more engaging lessons. We can (theoretically) keep up with grades.

But can we keep our students safe?

Teachers, administrators, and staff face the all-too-real battle of protecting students. We can make sure the door is locked. We can follow the safety procedures. We can pray, knowing life is full of circumstances beyond our control.

But we can't be crippled by the *what if* question. We lock the door and teach our students. We bring joy and passion to the classroom. We do what we can to protect them, and we teach them the best way we know how.

REFLECT: How can our faith take precedence over the fear when we think about keeping our students safe?

REFOCUS: Over and over again Scripture tells us, "Fear not." God must have meant it when he said it.

Heavenly Father,
Help us know how to protect our students. Help us recognize those students who need help and intervention before they get to the point of using violence. Help us teach without fear while being vigilant in keeping our students safe.
In Jesus' name,
Amen.

17

The Guinea Pig

> *A friend is always loyal, and a brother is born to help in time of need.*
> PROVERBS 17:17

I'd learned the hard way that guinea pigs bite. Hard. As an eager student teacher, I ignored the wisdom of my mentor teacher who declined to pet the show-and-tell critter. I stuck my hand in the cage and drew back a finger that needed a bandage and a tetanus shot.

A few months later, I was the substitute in a class with a pet guinea pig. The sounds coming from his cage were part moan and part howl. Something was wrong. He needed help, but I was *not* going in blindly this time.

"Does he always do this?" I asked the second-grade students.

"No, he's probably hungry," one student answered. "Our teacher hasn't been here for two days, and his food is locked in the cabinet."

My college classes hadn't covered how to quiet a hungry guinea pig. I couldn't ignore him, but I had no way to feed him. I couldn't imagine calling the office. *Hello, this is Mrs. Ruddell, the sub in Mrs. Smith's class. The guinea pig is crying. Can you help?*

I was certain that would get me uninvited from any future substitute jobs. Thankfully, the principal stopped by to check on me. "Mrs. Ruddell, how's everything going? Do you need anything?"

"Everything is great except the guinea pig. The kids think he's hungry. His food is locked in the cabinet."

I'm sure this wise, proactive principal thought she had seen and heard it all, but without missing a beat, she said, "I'll be right back." She returned with a guinea pig feast of lettuce and carrots. The part-moan, part-howl sound was replaced by the sound of contented chewing.

That principal was a problem-solver, well acquainted with "other duties as assigned." A hungry guinea pig did not faze her.

Sometimes we're not sure how to ask for help in the battleground moments. We can be thankful for the unexpected assistance that brings peace back to the classroom—even when the battle involves a guinea pig.

REFLECT: When have you needed help with a classroom situation but weren't quite sure how to ask?

_____
_____
_____
_____
_____
_____
_____
_____
_____
_____
_____
_____
_____
_____

THE GUINEA PIG 55

REFOCUS: Sometimes battleground wisdom is not having all the solutions but knowing when to ask for help. Watch for the helpers God sends. Offer help to others when you can.

Heavenly Father,
Thank you for always being aware of our needs. Thank you for sending help at just the right time. Help us to have the courage to ask for help when we need it. Keep us aware of those around us; let us see their needs and meet the ones we can.
In Jesus' name,
Amen.

18

The Countdown

> *I am counting on the Lord; yes, I am counting on him. I have put my hope in his word.*
>
> PSALM 130:5

I really should step up my game, I told myself as I walked from her room to mine. My hastily scribbled, often-not-updated number on the whiteboard paled in comparison to her elaborate, animated snowman on the screens.

But this moment of countdown creative envy left me with something deeper to ponder.

Does a countdown help or hurt?

A countdown can build excitement and anticipation, but one year a comment from a student stopped me in my tracks. "You can't wait to be away from us, can you?" She said it with a smile, but I wondered if that was what my countdown and my attitude were communicating to her.

In other words, my "check-attitude light" was on.

It wasn't the countdown itself that concerned me. It was my attitude: *I'd rather be anywhere but here.* Was my focus on how many days were left showing discontent?

Philippians 4:12 says, "I have learned the secret of being content in any and every situation." For teachers, this even includes the days before an extended break.

Checking out mentally and emotionally can contribute to battleground moments in the classroom. Sometimes a countdown can shift our focus to the future and cause us to miss playground moments in the present.

Realistically, there's nothing wrong with a fancy animated countdown or a handwritten one on the board. But when we allow discontent to dominate our thoughts, we can miss what God is doing in the present and lose the grace of trusting him for what he will do in the future.

REFLECT: How does a countdown challenge you?

REFOCUS: A change in routine is coming even if we don't know the countdown. God is faithful. We can count on him.

Heavenly Father,
Thank you for vacations, breaks, and days off. Thank you for the ability to look forward to a change in routine. Help us to count on you as we step into the classroom day after day, knowing you hold our days in the palm of your hand.
In Jesus' name,
Amen.

19

Aha Moments

> *For wisdom will enter your heart, and knowledge will fill you with joy.*
> PROVERBS 2:10

I passed?"

The student in my intervention class wasn't sure he heard me correctly; he wasn't used to passing tests. When I repeated, "Yes, you passed," his whole face lit up as he smiled from ear to ear. We celebrated with high fives, and I told him how proud I was of his hard work.

I *knew* he had been paying attention and working hard. I had listened as he explained his thinking and knew that he understood the math concepts we were studying. His barely passing grade took more work than a perfect score for some students. I was thrilled for him.

One of the best parts of teaching is seeing the eyes of our students light up. You see it when the little ones read a book for the first time. You see it when a student can explain something to one of their peers. For coaches, you see it when athletes experience success on the court or on the field.

When a student reaches a goal or has an academic achievement, their confidence is boosted. We teachers feel like proud parents. It's a joyful time. But what about the aha moments that aren't athletic or academic?

When a student trusts a teacher enough to ask for help or reaches out to help another student or makes a wise decision, we are also reminded of why we teach.

I wonder how our heavenly Father feels when he sees us have an aha moment. Does he smile when we understand something in his Word for the first time? Does he nod in approval when we respond to the nudge of the Holy Spirit? Does he pump his fist and say, "Yes!" when we share our story of his goodness with someone who needs to hear it?

Scripture tells us that God delights in us, and we can rest assured he loves aha moments too.

REFLECT: What is your favorite aha moment?

REFOCUS: Not every aha moment has a score attached. Celebrate even the small ones. Be encouraged by victories, even those that may not show up in the gradebook.

Heavenly Father,
Thank you for the encouragement we get from our students' aha moments. Thank you for the joy that comes from success after struggle. Show us how to lead our students to these moments, as you lead us to ours.
In Jesus' name,
Amen.

20

A New Semester

> *Put on your new nature, created to be like God—truly righteous and holy.*
> EPHESIANS 4:24

As I posted pictures of my classroom on social media, I smiled. The desk calendar was visible and on the right month. The top of the desk was shiny and clean. The piles of papers and materials soon taking over that surface hadn't formed yet. I knew it hadn't looked this clean since the first day of school and wouldn't again until the last. But at least for now, my soul felt the weightlessness of being caught up.

The start of a new semester is like a breath of fresh air. It's a gift that we know comes in the middle of the school year. Whatever pressure and stress weighed us down at the end of last semester has been erased like a marker on a whiteboard.

We march back into our classrooms with reignited inspiration to impact our students. We feel refreshed and rested, determined to make a difference. With fresh confidence, we can press on to the end of the school year.

No matter what battles came before, we have a new perspective to carry us through what is coming. In the first semester, we became students of those we teach, and learned things that will give us an edge in the second semester, as we look forward to the end of the year. We know the messy desk is coming. We know calendars will be covered in chaos. We know we will fall behind. But we also know the people entrusted to our care and classroom. This reset is one that comes with added grace.

We don't have to wait for a new semester to experience a restart with Jesus. When life has become a battleground, and the struggles of stress, sin, and shame are weighing us down, Jesus offers forgiveness, peace, and the strength to start again. All we have to do is ask him.

REFLECT: How can you give yourself the refreshment and relief of a new start?

REFOCUS: Clear off the desk. Get rid of the clutter. Let go of the old that's weighing you down and stealing your fresh start.

Heavenly Father,
Thank you for a new semester, a new beginning, and a chance to start again. Bless us as we enter this part of the school year. Renew our strength and stamina. Revive our love for this calling and for our students. Put a spring in our steps and put a smile on our faces as we enter the classroom each day. Keep the spark of new going as we press on through the semester. Give us delight in what we do and a glimpse of the impact we are making for eternity.
In Jesus' name,
Amen.

REFOCUS: Focus on the good more often than you do the difficult. Remind yourself of the things that put a smile on your face. Remember that the joy of the Lord is your strength.

Heavenly Father,
Thank you for the moments of joy we experience in teaching. Help us to focus on joy. And help us to keep the negative from clouding our vision, knowing we will find strength in its wake.
In Jesus' name,
Amen.

22

Parent Contacts

My child, listen and be wise: Keep your heart on the right course.
PROVERBS 23:19

"I can't believe you wouldn't let my son go to the bathroom. He's nearly a grown man, and he knows when he needs to go. I don't doubt that when *you* need to go, you just leave those kids in the classroom and go. When he says he needs to go, you need to let him!"

I resisted the urge to explain my personal bathroom schedule as she continued with her mom rant. I let her say her piece. Then it was my turn.

"Thank you for your concern. Here's my side of the story. In my experience, a student who needs to go to the restroom will quietly ask for permission. A student who stands up in the middle of my lecture and yells, 'I gotta go pee!' usually just wants to get out of class."

"He did that?"

"Yes, ma'am, he did."

"I'll take care of it." *Click.*

That student didn't ask to leave class to go to the bathroom again.

My first reaction when this mom lit into me was anger. I wanted to jump right in and explain my side of the story. But God put his hand over my mouth, and I listened first. Her perception was that her son had been treated unfairly. She was defending him. I heard her, then told her my side. She listened and then solved the problem.

It can be so tempting to jump in and prove that we're right and the student is wrong. Even when that is true, not hearing the parent out can escalate the situation.

There have been times when I've been in that angry mom's shoes. I've taken my child's side of the story as truth and gone into mama-bear mode. Our instinct is to protect our kids. That's true for the parents of our students too.

Working with parents can be a battle. Listening first is a good strategy for a win-win. A parent who feels heard may be more likely to listen and come to our aid.

REFLECT: When have you successfully de-escalated a situation with an upset parent?

REFOCUS: The goal of parent communication is to help the student succeed. Protective parents can come across as angry at teachers. Choosing professional over personal can de-escalate the situation.

Heavenly Father,
Give us wisdom as we communicate with parents for the good of our students. Give us the words to speak and the restraint to listen. Help us reassure parents that we are on their side and want what is best for their children.
In Jesus' name,
Amen.

23

Is the Door Locked? 2.0

> *Don't be afraid, for I am with you. Don't be discouraged,*
> *for I am your God. I will strengthen you and help you.*
> *I will hold you up with my victorious right hand.*
>
> ISAIAH 41:10

"We're going to have a lockdown drill today during fourth period," the voice over the intercom announced. Coming out of a brief retirement to teach eighth graders after the previous teacher had resigned, I knew I needed to know more.

"What corner do you go to when you have a lockdown drill?" I asked the students. They showed me the location, and I reminded them of our procedures. The door was locked, I turned off the lights, and we went to the corner and waited quietly until the drill was over.

These students were a dream. They did everything I asked them to the first time. When the drill began, they moved quietly. The boys huddled together, and the girls did the same, which made me laugh. My high schoolers wouldn't have done that.

As we waited, I heard footsteps in the hall. The administrators were checking classrooms to make sure the doors were locked, the lights were out, and the students couldn't be seen through the window in the door. I braced myself for the rattle of the door handle. Even though I knew it was a drill, I couldn't help but wonder *what if* all over again.

My students were as quiet as church mice. Quiet until they heard the doorknob being turned.

"Hello!" one of the boys shouted.

I motioned to keep him from saying anything else, while also trying to stifle my laughter. We then discussed the importance of remaining quiet during a lockdown. It doesn't do any good to hide if you're going to call out and let them know you're there.

But these are children. Thirteen- and fourteen-year-olds. They live with the reality of school shootings and lockdown drills, but they are children. Somebody was at the door, and this kid answered. He wasn't afraid.

God has given us the gift of laughter. It can bring much-needed levity to hard things like lockdown drills. I've heard it said that laughter is like a windshield wiper. It doesn't stop the rain, but it lets us see through it.

REFLECT: How have your students made you laugh in the middle of supposed-to-be-serious situations?

REFOCUS: Sometimes we need humor to lighten the moment. Fear can paralyze and steal our joy. Remember, it's only a drill.

Heavenly Father,
Thank you for the gift of laughter. Thank you for the relief it brings in the middle of challenging times. Thank you for the reminder to be joyful even in times that can be scary.
In Jesus' name,
Amen.

24

Meetings, Meetings, and More Meetings

> *"Everything is meaningless," says the Teacher, "completely meaningless!"*
> ECCLESIASTES 1:2

I stepped into my classroom and shut the door. *I've made it to my conference period.*

I would finally have time to sit at my desk, decompress, and prepare for the next class. I collapsed into my chair only to see a calendar pop up. "You have a meeting in two minutes."

There goes my relaxing planning period.

Meetings can often overwhelm us if we allow them. Sometimes it's difficult to see the difference they make, especially when there are immediate tasks that need to be addressed.

In this case, I needed to make more copies for my next class because first period ate theirs, I needed to take a bathroom break, and I needed to email a parent. But all of that would have to wait because I had forgotten about this meeting.

I grabbed my laptop and a pen, put a smile on my face, and hurried down the hall, knowing my frustration would have to stay behind. But the sheer number of meetings required in teaching can make us feel a little like Solomon when he wrote, "Everything is meaningless."

Fitting everything into the schedule is a battle. When we don't see the benefit, we might adopt our students' refrain: *When are we ever going to use this?* We may fail to see the bigger picture.

But as professionals, we can choose to perform even the parts of our job we don't like with a good attitude. If we are on our phones or being otherwise disrespectful to the speaker, we are behaving like our students—the ones we would scold.

Let's take the challenge to be professional. Let's bring the attitude we expect our students to possess. And let's avoid creating a battleground where there doesn't have to be one.

REFLECT: How do you respond to interruptions to your schedule?

REFOCUS: We can love our job without loving every part of it. Our attitudes and actions are a witness to others, especially in the not-so-fun parts of our job. Looking for joy in unexpected places shines a light into the darkest of rooms.

> *Heavenly Father,*
> *Thank you for the provision of a job and the satisfaction and benefits that it provides for us and for our families. Help us to perform all our job duties with joy and integrity. Help us to be productive and to accomplish our work even when the minutia of it feels burdensome.*
> *In Jesus' name,*
> *Amen.*

25

Celebrations

> *Always be full of joy in the Lord. I say it again—rejoice!*
> PHILIPPIANS 4:4

Everybody loves a party, right? Parties can lift our spirits. They can remind our hearts that joy exists even in the mundane. And they can draw people together in a way that might never happen otherwise.

One of my favorite principals understood the value of a good party. She brought an Easter-egg scramble and a marble contest, along with a field trip, as a reward to our high school campus. She also challenged students to transform half-hearted pep rallies into lively celebrations of school spirit that included everyone.

Students who had previously slumped in their seats in the gym stood and cheered. The excitement carried past the pep rallies. Students took turns singing the school song over the PA system when it was time for announcements. School was fun again.

She was the best I'd ever seen at creating positive school culture and making sure *all* students knew they were seen and valued. She had high expectations for students and teachers. But she also knew the value of celebration.

In my decades of teaching, I've seen music played during the passing period complete with teacher dance breaks. I've watched a young middle school teacher write notes of encouragement to her students before state testing and then celebrate big after it was over. I've seen a fellow math teacher and friend bring pie to celebrate Pi Day with his students.

We can all create playground moments and lessen the stress of battleground days with celebrations: high fives and fist bumps, special treats for holidays, and celebrations just because. They don't have to be big and fancy or expensive. There is a time for serious hard work, and there is a time to celebrate.

Scripture tells us to rejoice even in tough times. We can have playground moments even in the middle of the battle. Celebrations in the classroom can contribute to joy, and the joy of the Lord is our strength (Nehemiah 8:10).

REFLECT: How can you bring celebration to your classroom?

REFOCUS: Celebration is a way to show students we care. Celebration brings joy to the day. Celebration builds relationships that last.

Heavenly Father,
Thank you for the gift of celebration. Help us remember to celebrate with our students. Whether that is a fist bump on the way into class, a reminder that we are glad to see them, or an all-out party, may we be the first to join in.
In Jesus' name,
Amen.

26

In His Strength

> But he said to me, "My grace is sufficient for you, for my power is made perfect in weakness."
>
> 2 CORINTHIANS 12:9 (NIV)

It was the hardest day ever.

The adrenaline that had carried us through the day before was gone. The normally noisy campus gave way to an eerie silence. An army of counselors and support staff lined the halls to make sure any student or teacher who needed it had someone to talk to.

It all felt impossible.

Because what do you say the day after a student takes his own life in the school parking lot?

When the time came for me to address the class where the young man had been my student, I walked in accompanied by one of the counselors. I worried about this group. My relationship with this class bordered on adversarial. Most of them were more interested in getting the best of me than they were in learning algebra.

Even so, these were "my kids." They'd lost a friend. I knew no words would take away their pain, but it was important for me to let them know I cared. I began with "I'm so sorry for the loss of your friend."

We didn't do any math that day, but what we did was beyond important. We shared memories. We leaned on one another. We sat in quiet places together. It was and is the hardest place to be as a teacher—to watch your students hurt and not be able to fix it.

But we made it through the next couple of weeks, which brought a funeral, graduation, and the end of the school year. The atmosphere in class was one of support and encouragement. The lessons we learned in that short time transcended math.

We learned that relationships are important. We learned that life is short. We learned that when it came down to it, we cared about one another more than we realized.

Some battleground moments feel as though they might break us. It is scary and difficult to walk into a class where we know tragedy is waiting, and we may feel very small in the face of great big hurt. But when we don't have words that will fix a situation, we can offer our presence. When we can't take away our students' pain, we can give them space to process. When we feel incapable, we can offer them a capable God, one who will give us the strength to help carry them through all that feels impossible.

REFLECT: How do you help students deal with tragedy when your heart is breaking too?

_____
_____
_____
_____
_____
_____
_____
_____
_____

REFOCUS: God is faithful. He promises to be with us. We can trust him.

Heavenly Father,
Thank you for being capable when we are incapable. Thank you for your strength that is made perfect in our weakness. When we must lead our students through times of tragedy, give us wisdom. Give us words to say and, when needed, the wisdom to remain silent. Help us to lean on you in our own grief so that we can support our students in theirs.
In Jesus' name,
Amen.

27

An Eye-Opening Experience

> *The Lord is a shelter for the oppressed, a refuge in times of trouble.*
> PSALM 9:9

As the bell rang and kids began to take their seats, I greeted one of my favorite students. "We missed you yesterday. Where were you?"

"I had to meet with the principal at my sister's school," she replied.

Without a second thought, I asked, "Shouldn't your mom do that?"

"Mrs. Ruddell, my mom supports the bar. I support my mom."

Like many of our students at the alternative school, she had adult responsibilities at home. She was one of the few female students who didn't have a child yet, but she often functioned as a parent for her younger siblings.

Teaching these young people was eye-opening for me. Their normal was a world I had never navigated. My heart often wondered how these young people could even focus on school when life was so chaotic.

When students were new to our school, they were often cautious, even defensive. Most, however, figured out quickly that our school was a safe place. Motivated by positive attention, they worked hard to complete classes and gain credits toward graduation.

These young people shouldered adult situations, but in many ways they were still kids looking for someone who believed in them. We were surprised to see how hard they would work for something as simple as a sticker.

There were battleground moments and playground moments during my time teaching at the alternative school. I was often overwhelmed by the workload and the hard stories. But I was so proud of my students who overcame so much. The playground moments for me were building relationships with students and facing the challenge of motivating each one. Seeing them succeed in life was like extended recess.

When we carry hard things with our students, we are never nearer to the heart of the Father. Just as we care for our students and want to help them and guide them, our heavenly Father cares for us and wants to help us and guide us. We don't always know what our students need, but our Father always knows exactly what we need.

REFLECT: What has been your biggest eye-opening moment in teaching?

REFOCUS: A relationship with students is important. The stories behind the behavior help us help our students. Accept the challenge to inspire success in each student.

> *Heavenly Father,*
> *Help us to seek to understand our students. Show us how to hold them accountable, and teach them how to be successful, while also showing them that we care for them and about them.*
> *Let your love shine through us.*
> *In Jesus' name,*
> *Amen.*

28

Clifford the Big Red Dog Day

We can make our plans, but the Lord determines our steps.
PROVERBS 16:9

I smiled at the trail of big brown "paw prints" that stretched down the hallway and into the second-grade classroom. Headbands with big red ears were on each desk. A container of puppy chow waited to be devoured.

Everything was ready for Clifford the Big Red Dog's birthday party. After reading many of the books in the series, our students were ready to celebrate Clifford's birthday. I was a young student teacher, ready to assist my wise, experienced supervisor.

Early that morning the phone rang. "Michelle? My son has a fever. I'm not going to be there. There's no sub. You've got this."

I could scarcely believe that I was going to be on my own for such a momentous event. Truth be told, she had more confidence in me than I had in myself. I didn't want to let her down.

But the litany of doubt began to weigh heavily on me. *What if I forget something? Will it go smoothly? Can I manage the whole class in party mode all day?*

Visions of powdered-sugar puppy chow scattered everywhere and kids climbing over tables wearing ripped-up headbands swirled in my head. But as if my mentor could sense my growing anxiety, she talked me through the plan for the day, reminded me of key details, expressed her confidence in me, and proved to be my biggest cheerleader.

There were no major catastrophes. The headbands turned out fine. The kids and I enjoyed our day celebrating Clifford. After school, I smiled as I straightened the room and removed Clifford's paw prints from the floor. I felt like a teacher.

When our plans are interrupted, we anticipate a battle. We imagine the worst-case scenario. But then we adapt and adjust. We enjoy the moment. The unexpected becomes a playground moment instead of the battle we feared.

REFLECT: When have you had a change of plans that pushed you out of your comfort zone?

_____
_____
_____
_____
_____
_____
_____
_____
_____
_____
_____

REFOCUS: Know that plans will change. Listen to the encouragers. Enjoy the unexpected.

*Heavenly Father,
Thank you for courage and strength to handle the unexpected. Thank you for your perfect plan, which always prevails. Give us strength to walk in confidence and obedience to you.
In Jesus' name,
Amen.*

29

Change in the Weather

> *As long as the earth remains, there will be planting and harvest, cold and heat, summer and winter, day and night.*
>
> GENESIS 8:22

The full moon glowed, and the wind blew cold.

This double whammy alone had me questioning my lesson plans for the day. I could get students up and moving to harness the weather-related energy, or I could assign work that would keep them in their seats with a grade attached for incentive. I just needed to get through today with some sanity remaining.

I'll admit to thinking my college professor was crazy when he said, "Be sure to watch the weather. It will affect your students' behavior." But when I had a classroom of my own, I saw the wisdom in his advice firsthand.

Even in Texas, where our winters are mostly mild, January could bring a tough weather stretch. The classroom buzzed with the buildup of energy caused by days of indoor recess. Teenagers wearing shorts and crocs on a below-freezing day complained about being cold. The thermostats on the wall served no purpose other than decoration. Every notification on our phone brought hope of a snow day. Teachers and students alike were craving sunshine and fresh air.

Fronts, full moons, or freezing temperatures can create battleground moments. It can be hard to discover the playground moments when we're stuck inside. If there was a one-size-fits-all, works-every-time answer for that, we'd all be sitting pretty—but there's not. Sometimes it works to switch up the routine, sometimes it's better to stick to what's familiar and expected. What worked best for me was to anticipate the elevated energy in the classroom and roll with the punches.

Remember, even in life, seasons change. The moon won't stay full, the cold front will blow through, and winter doesn't last forever. Hold on to that hope always.

REFLECT: What has worked for you in your classroom on change-in-the-weather days?

_____
_____
_____
_____
_____
_____
_____
_____
_____
_____
_____
_____

REFOCUS: There is joy even in weather-related chaos. Flexibility with plans and expectations helps us find that joy. Embrace each season as it comes.

Heavenly Father,
Thank you for changing seasons. Thank you for the hope that comes from knowing that winter doesn't last forever. Show us how to embrace each season as it comes, and how to find joy in that season as we march toward the next one.
In Jesus' name,
Amen.

30

Back to the Basics

> *Get all the advice and instruction you can, so you will be wise the rest of your life.*
> PROVERBS 19:20

Manuel was a husband, a father, and my student. Determined to graduate from high school so he could be a better provider for his family, he found himself struggling to pass the state test in math, which was a graduation requirement. As he and I worked through practice problems, I noticed something interesting.

Manuel understood the problems. He could describe the process of solving them. His struggle? Basic math operations. We ditched the practice problems and worked on basic arithmetic. His confidence soared. He passed the test. He graduated.

Seeing students succeed and gain confidence is one of the best job perks of teaching. In the classroom and out, sometimes we benefit from going back to the basics.

Recently, I noticed that my daily quiet time was causing me stress. I was behind in my reading plan, a devotional, and a Bible study. I knew something wasn't right if I was stressed about opening my Bible because I was behind.

Just like Manuel, I went back to basics. I sat down with my Bible, a pen, and a journal. No workbook, no podcast, and no published reading plan. I decided I would pray, read, and copy Scripture. Writing the verses down helped me focus and prevented rabbit chasing. It slowed me down enough to concentrate on what I'd read.

Now my morning quiet time is less stressful. I look forward to spending time in God's Word, rather than trying to rush and play catch-up. Going back to the basics has been good for me and proves that what is often good for our students is good for us as well.

REFLECT: When has there been a time when you or your students would have benefited from going back to the basics?

REFOCUS: Sometimes a focus on the basics is just what teachers and students need. Filling gaps for students increases their confidence and their success. Student success turns the battleground into a playground.

Heavenly Father,
Thank you that faith in Jesus is simple. Help us to know in teaching and in life when we need to go back to the basics. Show us how to trust you and not to overcomplicate things.
In Jesus' name,
Amen.

31

Teacher Time Warp

> *Then Jesus said, "Come to me, all of you who are weary and carry heavy burdens, and I will give you rest."*
>
> MATTHEW 11:28

Have a marvelous, meeting-filled Monday!"

My usual text of encouragement drew my friend's playful reply, "Today is *Tuesday*, silly!"

Even I chuckled at my mistake. It was hard for me to believe I could get that mixed up. But so many things can throw us off to the point we aren't sure what day it is, or we are sure—but only to be proven wrong: Dinner with church friends on *Monday* night, which made it feel like Sunday. Testing week at school, which throws everything off. Jeans week—who cares what day it is when we get to wear jeans?

Long weekends, extended breaks, and summer—they can all contribute to what-day-is-it syndrome.

During the school year, we have a set schedule and bells that tell us when to start, when to change classes, and in an ideal world, when to go home. Routines make it easier to remember what day it is. Many of us will have the day and date posted somewhere in our classrooms, and we can even delude ourselves that it's only for the students.

But what about when there are no bells because we aren't in school? Is today Tuesday, Wednesday, or Saturday? Who knows?

There's glorious freedom during the summer time warp until July, when panic sets in. Then the back-to-school email from the district arrives in our inbox. This year becomes last year. Next year jumps to the distant future. That's the teacher time warp.

I love that our chosen profession has a built-in rest and reset. The sprint from spring break to the end of the school year is an exercise in exhaustion. Summer brings the chance to rest, refresh, and recharge.

Even beyond the school walls, rest and a reset are beneficial. From a walk or a brain break to a full-blown retreat, time to recharge can restore a positive outlook, so we're ready to resume what a routine demands.

REFLECT: What do you do during school breaks to rest and recharge?

REFOCUS: Rest is important. Time away from the routine is needed. Recharge and refresh for the routine ahead.

Heavenly Father,
Thank you for the breaks our profession provides, allowing us a rest from the day-to-day routine. Thank you for the chance to recharge our energy and our patience. Thank you for a built-in restart and the peace new beginnings provide.
In Jesus' name,
Amen.

32

The Plan

> *"For I know the plans I have for you," says the Lord. "They are plans for good and not for disaster, to give you a future and a hope."*
> JEREMIAH 29:11

When I was a child, my stuffed animals were the smartest ones on the block. I spent hours mimicking my teachers as I taught my "students," no doubt because academics came easily for me and school was my favorite place to be. It gave me the acceptance and approval I craved and sparked my dream of becoming a teacher one day.

In those years, I imagined a classroom full of elementary-aged students, as attentive as the stuffed animals in my first class. I had a plan, but God's plan was different. I began my teaching career at an alternative school teaching what was then called home economics.

The next twenty-six years of God's plan had me teaching middle and high school math. My students were both more of a challenge and more of a delight than my stuffed-animal pupils. I can also say God's plan was better than mine.

As teachers, so many things can alter our plans. Schedule changes, bad-weather days, and field trips call for adjustments. Policies, personnel, and priorities change. Just when we've got into a rhythm that works, the rules of the game change and we must align our plans with them.

The same thing is true in life. All through Scripture we see where God interrupts the plans of people he used to accomplish his purpose.

Noah never planned to build an ark. As a young shepherd, David never thought he would be king. The woman at the well hadn't planned to meet the Messiah.

When plans change, our response can determine whether the change creates a battleground or a playground. We can resist and complain, or we can adjust and adapt. We get to choose who we want to be.

God's plans are better than ours. We can trust him to hold the bigger picture. But we must walk in obedience one step at a time.

REFLECT: How do you respond when the plans change?

REFOCUS: Change is a certainty. Jesus is constant. And God is worthy of our trust.

Heavenly Father,
Thank you for orchestrating the details of our lives. Thank you for having a plan for us. Teach us to hear your voice and to follow you each step of the way.
In Jesus' name,
Amen.

33

Parent Contacts 2.0

A cheerful look brings joy to the heart; good news makes for good health.
PROVERBS 15:30

Who has time for this?
I'll freely admit that was my first thought when an administrator announced we'd be required to make positive contacts. I was skeptical. I thought it was a waste of precious time. But then I did what I was told, and I was left amazed.

"Tanner did a really good job in class today. I appreciate his attitude and effort."

"I want to brag on Maddie. She has really been working hard and is making great progress."

"Allie always contributes to class discussion. I'm so glad to have her in class."

I didn't wince as I hit Send on these emails. I didn't cross my fingers hoping the phone call would go straight to voicemail. I didn't fear the possibility of angry and defensive reactions.

These contacts were fun to make. The parents were often surprised to get good news from school. And when I later had to address issues with grades or behavior with the same parents, they were much more receptive because we already had a connection.

I mean, what parent doesn't want to hear the teacher notice the good in their child and not only the things that need improvement?

When I served as a teacher leader, we were trained to coach teachers. We were taught to note something positive, as well as an area for growth. It's a solid model. Yet there were times when I wanted to be able to just tell the teachers I coached, *That was fabulous. Your students responded well. Good job. Period.*

We all like to be acknowledged for working hard at our jobs. The same is true for our students. We should brag about them when we have the chance.

Relationships and communication with parents can be battleground moments. Laying groundwork with positive communication can make parents allies, rather than opponents.

REFLECT: How can you incorporate positive contacts into your communication routine?

REFOCUS: Acknowledge and communicate the positive. Be in the business of bragging on students. Be as vocal about the good as you are with the bad.

Heavenly Father,
Thank you for the ability and the opportunity to collaborate with parents in the education of their children. Guide us in our communication with them. Help us to recognize and voice the positives and to show the parents that we care about their children.
In Jesus' name,
Amen.

34

A Clean Slate

He has removed our sins as far from us as the east is from the west.
PSALM 103:12

What makes this kid tick? I wondered. Office referrals didn't faze him. Phone calls to his mother had little effect. The best I could do was sit him in the back corner of the room so he didn't have an audience.

Nothing I had in my teacher's bag of tricks had worked. He was intelligent. His grades were good even when his behavior was not. He was in my class two years in a row, for two separate math courses. By the end of the second year, we were left simply tolerating each other.

The teacher tool I sharpened the most during those two years was the importance of a clean slate. Every day when that young man walked through the door of my classroom, we started over—even when he was returning after his behavior had earned an in-school suspension.

"I'm glad you're back. Let's have a good day." Sometimes this was a mere fake-it-till-you-make-it greeting.

"It's good to see you. Do you understand my expectations for your classroom behavior?" This one came with experience. It helped to review expectations before that student entered the classroom.

"Good morning. Are you ready for a good day?" Showing a student that they were seen and that I was not holding the previous day's actions against them helped the student, and it helped me.

I learned to apply it to other students as well. The weight of keeping score of past offenses is heavy. No teacher has time for that.

Offering students and coworkers new mercies is a good battleground strategy. Keeping score and holding grudges can steal our joy. Remembering how much we have been forgiven, we then hold the capacity to also forgive.

REFLECT: How can you communicate the concept of a clean slate to students?

REFOCUS: Keeping score of past offenses is a heavy burden. Lighten the load by offering a clean slate. Forgive as you have been forgiven.

Heavenly Father,
Thank you for the gift of forgiveness and a clean slate. When we are tempted to keep score or keep our guard up because of previous offenses, remind us that you have removed our sins as far as the east is from the west. Help us to forgive others as you have forgiven us.
In Jesus' name,
Amen.

35

Jesus as Teacher

> *They discussed this among themselves and said,*
> *"It is because we didn't bring any bread."*
>
> MATTHEW 16:7 (NIV)

Nowhere do we understand the heart of a teacher more than looking to Jesus himself.

I was reminded of this one night during Bible study as we read that Jesus warned his disciples about the religious leaders of the day. "Be on your guard against the yeast of the Pharisees and the Sadducees" (Matthew 16:6).

But I laughed aloud at the disciples' comment in the next verse: "It's because we didn't bring any bread." These darling disciples sound like my students. Sometimes they missed the whole point.

The disciples had seen Jesus feed more than five thousand people with five loaves and two fish. Bread wasn't the issue. The disciples had witnessed healing. They had heard Jesus teach and traveled with him. But they totally missed his warning about the religious leaders they would encounter.

Have you ever had the best lesson, the best questions, the most fabulous example, yet your students missed the point? Jesus understands. He was the perfect teacher, yet his disciples thought he was talking about bread instead of issuing a warning. On another occasion they argued about who was the greatest of them all. (Anyone teach middle school boys?)

Unlike Jesus, we aren't perfect teachers. When our students miss the point of our lessons, it might be our fault. Maybe we misjudged their prior knowledge. Maybe we didn't communicate clearly. Or maybe, they just didn't get it.

We may even respond like Jesus did in Matthew 16:9 and 11. "Do you still not understand?" or "How is it that you don't understand that I wasn't talking to you about bread?"

Jesus reminded his students of what they had seen. He reminded them of his feedings of the five thousand and of the four thousand. He led them to the conclusion: *It's not about the bread.*

When we are frustrated with our students' lack of understanding, we can remember that Jesus was a teacher too. He gets it. We can turn a battleground moment into a playground moment when we realize that even Jesus' students sometimes missed the point.

REFLECT: When have you been surprised that your students missed the point of the lesson?

REFOCUS: Sometimes students miss the point. Maybe it's us, maybe it's them. But remember, it happens to the best of us.

Heavenly Father,
Thank you for the connection we teachers have to Jesus. Help us look to him as our example. Show us how to teach as he teaches and love like he loves.
In Jesus' name,
Amen.

36

I Messed Up

> *Godly sorrow brings repentance that leads to salvation and leaves no regret, but worldly sorrow brings death.*
>
> 2 CORINTHIANS 7:10 (NIV)

My patience was gone.

My class, which consisted mostly of freshman male athletes, was winning a rousing game of push the teacher's buttons. One smart-aleck comment sent me over the edge. I snarkily replied to him with a phrase best translated into *intelligent donkey*.

The gasp from my students nearly removed all our breathable air. My heart sank. *What had I done?*

My apology followed so quickly it was probably a run-on sentence. "I should never, ever use that language, especially in the classroom. I am sorry for losing my temper."

There was no excuse for my reply to him. It was completely inappropriate on my part. It didn't matter what he had said to me. I was wrong.

As soon as class was over, I headed for the principal's office. With each step, I wondered what it was like to be fired. I timidly knocked on his office door.

The door had barely closed behind me when I said, "Your phone is probably going to start ringing."

He looked concerned. "What happened?"

I told him about the class. I told him about the student's comment. Then I told him what I said.

He didn't say anything but looked at me as if he expected there to be more to the story. A look of relief spread across his face. "Oh, is that all?"

Still certain that I was going to be fired, I responded, "That's it."

"Don't worry. We've all lost our temper at some point. You've apologized and probably got their attention."

In twenty-six years of teaching, I lost my temper in that way only one other time. It happened to be with a school board member's son in a year when all our administrators were new to the district.

Just as before, I was certain I would be fired, especially as they didn't know that this wasn't my typical behavior or vocabulary. I went to my friend who was a counselor on our campus and told her what I'd done. She suggested that I call the parents and apologize. I did just that, and I didn't get fired.

Battleground moments happen when dealing with students. Sometimes we mess up. A good strategy is to admit what we did, apologize, and do better.

REFLECT: How do you handle the mistakes you make in the classroom?

REFOCUS: There has been only one perfect teacher. The rest of us will make mistakes. But when we respond honestly, we can win the battle.

Heavenly Father,
Guide every word and action we take in and out of the classroom. Direct our thoughts and our words. When we mess up, give us the courage and the integrity to apologize and strive to do better. Help us to extend grace to students, parents, and coworkers alike.
In Jesus' name,
Amen.

37

Overwhelmed

We are hard pressed on every side, but not crushed; perplexed, but not in despair; persecuted, but not abandoned; struck down, but not destroyed.

2 CORINTHIANS 4:8–9 (NIV)

Will I ever get it all done?

Recording video lessons for remote learning. Answering emails with questions from students, parents, and coworkers. Grading assignments. Coordinating lesson plans and paper packets for our high school math team.

Teaching in the spring of 2020 gave new meaning to the sentence *I'm building the plane while flying.*

Even though prepandemic teacher duties had left me drowning at times, this was different. The COVID shutdown brought a whole new level of being overwhelmed, and everyone was stressed. Not only a grade level or a department. Not only one campus. Not only a few families. *Everybody.* No one was left for those who were struggling.

Added to school stress was the adjustment to being at home all the time. No more classes full of students or in-person conversations with coworkers. Church services were online. Groceries were picked up curbside. Like many, I began to feel an emotional downward spiral. I craved the energy I get from being around real live people.

What can I do? Everyone is stressed because of this pandemic.

Knowing gratitude had been my go-to when I was sad, depressed, or just having a pity party, I started a list.

1) I am thankful for a safe, warm home.
2) I am thankful for a job where I can keep working and for which I will continue to get paid.
3) I am thankful that our district was ahead of the game with technology.
4) I am thankful that my kids are out of school so that I'm not trying to teach remotely and supervise my kids' at-home learning.

When *nothing* was normal, I looked back at other times in my life when my routine had been shaken. I've experienced divorce, the death of a child, and health struggles with my daughters. But in every circumstance, one thing has remained the same. Jesus is the same, yesterday, today, and forever. None of the COVID madness was a surprise to him, and nothing we face is beyond his reach.

REFLECT: When have you felt God's presence and strength in the middle of overwhelming circumstances?

REFOCUS: Remember, God is our refuge and our strength. His grace is sufficient. His peace transcends understanding.

Heavenly Father,
Thank you for always being present for us, even when we are overwhelmed by responsibilities and world events. Give us strength each day to do what you would have us do. Continue to be our peace in times of chaos.
In Jesus' name,
Amen.

38

Summer School

Do not be anxious about anything, but in every situation, by prayer and petition, with thanksgiving, present your requests to God.

PHILIPPIANS 4:6 (NIV)

"Come see me during your planning period."

As I read these seven words from my principal, Mr. VanCleave, fear struck my heart. I spent all day contemplating what I'd done wrong and even began imagining my career choices after I'd been fired. By the time my conference period rolled around, I was a nervous wreck.

"Michelle, we are looking for summer-school teachers. Are you interested?"

I sighed like the air going out of a balloon. Why couldn't the email have said, "Do you want to teach summer school?"

But after spending my day thinking about how to brush up on my burger-flipping skills to earn extra summer income, I agreed summer school was a much better option. Even as I told Mr. VanCleave yes, I relaxed because I still had a job.

Once summer arrived, I rode the emotional roller coaster from *I'm going to get fired* to *I've got the highest-paying summer job I've ever had*. There were other benefits to teaching summer school that I didn't even realize until later.

Getting to know students in a smaller summer-school setting made it much easier when they came into my class in the regular school year;

we already had established a relationship. Summer school was also a great place to try new activities and brainstorm for the new school year.

When I read the email that morning, I envisioned being jobless. But what was waiting was a blessing. I had spent all day worrying over something that wasn't even reality.

Worry is a joy stealer. It creates battlegrounds where there are none. The Bible says, "Do not be anxious about anything." We can replace worry with our trust in a faithful God, who provides for all our needs.

REFLECT: How have you allowed worry to steal your joy?

REFOCUS: Scripture says not to worry about anything. Present your requests to God. Remember how he has been faithful in the past.

Heavenly Father,
Thank you for Scripture that reminds us to not be anxious. Help us to remember how you have worked in the past, to see how you are working in the present, and to trust you to work in the future. Thank you for providing for us beyond our wildest imagination.
In Jesus' name,
Amen.

39

Summer School 2.0

> *Two people are better off than one, for they can help each other succeed. If one person falls, the other can reach out and help. But someone who falls alone is in real trouble.*
>
> ECCLESIASTES 4:9

Flipping burgers has to be easier than this summer-school gig, I thought. Seriously doubting the extra money was worth the chaos, I looked at twenty-five students in the computer lab. There was no way to help one student with their work without turning my back on the other twenty-four.

I knew it was a recipe for disaster. I could either try to teach students as they worked through their self-paced computer program for the course they were working on, or I could focus on crowd control. But I could not do both.

I survived that session feeling like a failure with new thoughts swirling around in my head:

A good teacher would have figured out how to make it work.

A good teacher would have been able to teach and *monitor*.

A good teacher would have been able to motivate these students.

I started the new school year embarrassed at how the summer had gone. My patience and my confidence were depleted. I was sure my coworkers and administrators knew I was a horrible teacher.

I later gained the courage to share the story of that summer disaster with a few teacher friends. I discovered that it was not that I was a horrible teacher. It was a bad setup with a disastrous combination of students. Administrators listened. Summer school was different from then on.

It's not easy to let others know when we are struggling. We wonder what they will think about us or what they will say to others. In teaching, it's easy to isolate ourselves. We stay in our rooms and talk to other teachers only during the passing period. We compare our teaching to what we think others are like.

We may feel like we come up short. We can turn this battleground moment into a playground moment by communicating with other teachers and administrators when we struggle. Battles are easier when we fight them together.

REFLECT: Have you ever felt like a failure as a teacher and been afraid to let anyone know?

REFOCUS: Classroom disasters can result from things outside the teacher's control. We might feel like the only goal is to survive and advance to the next day. But speaking up and reaching out will help us survive in the long term.

Heavenly Father,
Thank you for the calling you have placed on us to educate children. Sustain us on the rough days. Give us courage and wisdom to handle difficulties. Show us who we can talk to and where we can go for help.
In Jesus' name,
Amen.

40

Francisco 2.0

May the God of hope fill you with all joy and peace as you trust in him, so that you may overflow with hope by the power of the Holy Spirit.
ROMANS 15:13 (NIV)

Remember Francisco? The one who was tired of wearing his ankle monitor? The one who led me to ask God if he was sure I was in the right place? The one who became one of my favorite students ever?

Success with Francisco came in small steps. We focused on the positive because he had encountered so much negative, which had done nothing to help him succeed.

When he had a rough day or a rough class period, we started over with a clean slate. I stretched my brain to learn new ways to help him focus. Our curriculum was self-paced. Francisco was finishing courses and earning credits toward graduation.

By Christmas that year, the principal said, "You have managed to get Francisco to work more than his other teachers. We are going to put him in your room all day."

No way. Forty-five minutes at a time was more than enough for me. I didn't think I could keep him focused all day.

Truthfully, I was afraid my success with Francisco was about to go out the window. I explained to the principal that it already took great effort to keep him focused and working. I didn't think putting him in the same classroom all day was a good idea.

The principal put him in there anyway.

In education and in life, we don't always get to decide how things are done. I worked with Francisco all day long for the remainder of the year. It wasn't easy. But we both survived the year.

Francisco made progress toward graduation, and I learned so much about keeping students engaged and motivating them to keep working. I consider his progress one of my greatest achievements as a teacher.

I'll never forget his entrance into my classroom for the first time or his surprise when I let him do his work sitting on top of the dryer in our home economics classroom. Teaching Francisco gave me a glimpse of what education is all about: meeting the needs of students and finding ways to help them be successful.

Educating children is the most exhausting, rewarding calling we can answer. If we're not careful, the battleground moments of this job can make us strained, stressed, and snappy. They can affect our physical and mental health. But even on the days when difficulty outweighs the delight, our students are worth the fight.

The successes. The aha moments. The good decisions. Hearing our name called from a grocery store aisle or across the restaurant as if we were rock stars. There's nothing like it.

We wanted to change the world, and by his grace, we're doing it one student at a time.

REFLECT: What is your favorite student success story?

_____

_____

_____

_____

_____

REFOCUS: Look for the good in every student. Find ways to connect. Celebrate success.

> *Heavenly Father,*
> *Thank you for both the battleground and the playground. Be with us in this battle. Give us strength, give us joy, and give us courage. Help us to see our students as you see us—beloved, worthy, and called to hope and a future.*
> *In Jesus' name,*
> *Amen.*

A Blessing for the Battleground

May your playground moments far outnumber your battleground ones.

May your class sizes be small and your planning periods long. May you find a teacher-bestie and a coffee cup that never runs dry. May your word walls gleam and your heart hold on to the excitement of a new year.

May your days all feel like Friday and your months like August. May technology never fail and the copier stay jam-free. May your paycheck stretch like loaves and fishes and your heart stay open to new ideas.

May you know God's joy on good days. May you know his strength on hard days. May you know his grace on messy days. But may you know every day that what you do matters for eternity.

May you be encouraged to keep moving forward despite the circumstances. May you reflect the light of Jesus no matter where he calls you. May you experience his deepest blessing as you bravely give to so many, one battle at a time.

From the playground to the battleground, God be with you.

About the Author

MICHELLE RUDDELL, a retired educator turned author, brings decades of teaching experience to her writing. With degrees in education and multiple certifications, she now inspires others through books and speaking engagements. Michelle has contributed to several anthologies, including *Stories of Roaring Faith, Volume Three* (Roaring Lambs Publishing), *We Get You, God Is Faithful,* and *Trusting God* (Redemption Press). She self-published *Welcome to the Club, I'm Sorry You're Here: Hope for Grieving Parents,* available on Amazon. Her unique blend of educational expertise and faith-based perspective offers readers a practical approach to life's challenges. Michelle's latest work, *From the Playground to the Battleground*, continues her mission of providing encouragement and guidance in education and faith.

www.ingramcontent.com/pod-product-compliance
Lightning Source LLC
Chambersburg PA
CBHW050239030825
30445CB00006B/30